MW01231541

STOCK MARKET

INVESTING

A Crash Course Guide to Trading from
Beginners to Expert:
How to Create Passive Income to Get
Fresh Money to Buy and Sell Options

Anthony Sinclair

2

Table of Contents

5

Introduction

The fact is that for most young people, investing might not be the most important thing in their lives. Until they get older and established in a career, saving and investing for retirement may not be at the top of their priority list; there are other things that might seem more pressing and exciting at this stage in life.

When you're young, you have limited resources to invest. You're also still trying to figure out who you are — what kind of career or education you want to pursue, and how much risk you want to take with your money. For these reasons, it's not a good idea to jump into the stock market before you have a better handle on your financial circumstances and goals.

This doesn't mean you'll never be able to invest in the stock market, but it does mean that you're a long way off from making a decision that will have a major impact on your life. Until then, there are plenty of other ways to get started with investing and he stock market without getting ahead of yourself.

It is difficult to believe there was a time when the stock market didn't exist. The stock market is on the tip of nearly everyone's tongue. Even individuals who do not invest at least know it exists. It is largely understood that the New York Stock Exchange is the biggest market of them all, with any company listed on it that wants to be recognized globally. However, how did the stock market come to fruition? Is there more than the NYSE (New York Stock Exchange)? There are more exchanges and it started with the Real Merchants of Venice and British Coffeehouses.

Europe was filled with moneylenders that filled in the gaps of the larger banks. Moneylenders would trade between themselves. One lender might get rid of a high-risk, high-interest loan by trading it to another lender. Moneylenders also purchased government debt. In a natural evolution, lenders started selling debts to customers who were looking to invest.

Investors also put their money into ships and crews. Most of the time-limited liability companies would go on a single voyage to gain merchandise from Asia and the East Indies as a way to bring a profit to the investor. New companies were usually formed for the next voyage to reduce the risk of investing in ships that could end up in disaster. The East India companies worked with investors by providing dividends made from the goods that came in. Stocks were now in place, where the first joint-stock company was created. At the time, there were royal charters that made competition impossible and thus, investors gained huge profits.

It was not without its troubles. The stock market is based on economic stability. When instability reigns the stock market can crash because there is no liquidity, which is what happened during the Great Depression. Everyone saw the banks failing due to debts and little liquidity, which in turn caused others to suffer, businesses too close, and stock shares to plummet.

The stock market formed from a need to have a place to conduct the business of selling shares, which was already happening. Governments needed to regulate stock sales, and prevent issues like the SSC crash. Nevertheless, there was also greed on behalf of wealthy citizens. There was a clear way to earn money from someone else's labor, thus the stock exchanges were started.

Investors and traders sell stocks after the IPO based on the perceived value. A company's value can go up or down, which is where investors make their money. A company's stock price that rises can provide a profit. If an investor has purchased those shares and the price or company value decreases, then the investor will lose money. In addition, the investors and traders will push the price in an up or down direction.

Investors have one of two goals: investing in the short or the long term. A long-term investment is based on a stock continuing to rise in price. A short-term investment is to gain quick cash and pulling out before the stock price decreases.

Mature companies offer dividends to their shareholders. If you have stocks, then you are a shareholder in a company. If you hold the stocks long enough and have enough stock in a company, you can vote on new board members. Dividends are company profits that you get a cut of.

Investors will make money on the price fluctuations and the dividends. A seller is often trying to gain a profit by selling to a new buyer. The new buyer is also trying to buy as low as possible so that when the stock price continues to increase, they will make a profit.

The profit is calculated by taking the initial buy price and subtracting it from the closing or sale price. For example, if you buy into Google at $400 and wait for it to go up to $600, then the profit is $200 per share.

Sellers can push the price down due to supply and demand. This financial market works based on supply and demand.

You should already know that in economics when there is an oversupply of a product, the price is low. There is no demand for the product; therefore, a company or in this case a stock is not of interest.

When there is an undersupply of something like a stock, the demand is high. With more interested parties, the price will continue to increase.

If there is an even amount of supply and demand, then equality exists and there is no movement to see.

For the stock market, when too many people sell a stock, the price will decline. When too many people buy a stock, the price will continue to rise. If there is an equal number of shares and interest, then the price usually trades sideways because there is a balance.

As you learn about the stock market, you will hear the word volume, often. Volume is the number of shares that change hands on a daily basis. Millions of shares can be traded on the stock exchange in a day as investors attempt to make money from increasing or decreasing prices.

The stock market works based on the interest or volume of traders. If a stock does not have any volume or very little, then it is not being actively traded, thus the price is not moving. Traders such as market makers get into the market in order to buy or sell stocks for companies with low volume. They do not stop a stock from rising or falling. Instead, market makers just trying to garner interest in the company's stock.

When it comes to the stock market and traders, most individuals are looking for high-volume traders, with fluctuating prices. They get in, make a profit, and get out finding the next big profit.

BEGINNERS

Chapter 1. The Basics of Investing in Stocks

Delayed gratification is a strong suit that few have and this is why investing has always been a challenge for many. You want to make money but not in a decade or a couple of years, but right now. Ponzi schemes aside, profitable investments that can actually build you wealth for a lifetime take time and lots of patience. These two things are probably the most important tools that any beginner in stock market investing needs to be aware of.

Our motivations for investing may differ but ultimately all investments have one goal in common; to make a return or profit on the investment. You may be eyeing early retirement, you may be in it for financial freedom or maybe you are just sick of having your money sitting in a savings account attracting point nothing interest. Regardless of what your goals are, the idea behind investing is that you use your money to make more money.

The stock market presents a unique opportunity for both retail and corporate investors because anyone can do it at any scale. You can invest as little as $1000 or as much as a million dollars. There are room and opportunity for everyone to get in and make a decent return on their investment. That said, the stock market is not the way to go if you want quick money. Stocks like most other investments have one thing in common; they depend on the power of time.

Time is your biggest ally when it comes to investing. If you have been waiting for a magical moment when you will have "enough" money to start investing, the bad news is that you will probably never have "enough" money and the other bad news is that the right time to start investing was yesterday.

A common misconception that most people have is that you need to have a lot of money to start investing. In actual fact, people who invest do not necessarily have more money than you, they simply make investing a priority. And because they make investing a priority, they end up having more money than you. See how that works?

Unlike consumption, investment takes money out of your pocket and puts it towards your future. When you can think of investment as an insurance policy to safeguard your financial future then the decision on when and if to invest becomes pretty much a no-brainer. Nobody wants to be cash strapped forever or have to work themselves to the grave because they did not put their money to work when they had the chance.

The beauty of this golden age of technology that we live in is that anyone with the will and determination to do so can access all the tools they need to start investing in the stock market. This ease of accessibility coupled with its affordability has made the stock market increasingly popular with retail investors. With just a few a hundred dollars you can find an online brokerage at the click of a button and get started as an investor in the stock market. Yes, it is that easy. Before you jump on the bandwagon, however, it is important to understand what you are investing in. The natural starting point is, of course, understanding how the stock market works.

How Does the Stock Market Work?

It is no coincidence that most people who have wealth have a big part of this wealth invested in stocks. Stocks carry their fair share of risks for any investor but when done right, stock market investing can be one of the most efficient ways to build and retain wealth.

A stock market is an exchange where people trade by buying and selling shares on traded companies. Once you have bought shares in a company your stock gives you ownership of a small part of that company. With this ownership, the value of your investment will be determined by the movements of the price of the company's shares. If for instance, you bought Apple stocks and the price moves up while you are holding the stock then the value of your investment increases. On the other hand, if the price of the Apple stocks decreases while you are holding the stocks, the value of your investment decreases.

The price of a stock is driven by the forces of supply and demand. Naturally, when the demand for a particular stock is higher than the supply, the price of that stock will increase. In much the same way, when the supply is higher than the demand, then the price of that stock will decrease. In essence, the stock price is a reflection of the value as set by the market conditions. When you buy a stock as an investor, your general goal is to make money when the price of the stock increases. This is why a big part of investing in the stock market is knowing how to select the right stocks to buy.

When the price of the shares you have appreciates, you can sell your shares at a profit. This means that you will get a return on your investment and you can reinvest your capital back into the market or you can cash out. The beauty of stock market investing is that there is usually no limit to how long you can hold your investment. You can keep your shares for 20 years or you can choose to sell them when the share price appreciates. This will ultimately depend on what your end goal is.

Price appreciation is not the only way to make money in the stock market. Dividends are payments made out to shareholders when a company makes a profit. This means that depending on the type of shares you have, you will receive dividends from the company whose shares you hold.

For instance, if you bought Tesla stocks and the company pays out dividends quarterly to their shareholders, you will get a percentage of these dividends based on the value of your shares. You can choose to take these dividends as a cash payment or you can choose to reinvest them back into the company by buying more shares.

It is important to note that not all companies pay dividends. This means that if you want to make money in the stock market by earning regular dividends, you will need to understand the type of stocks to buy and which company's stocks will get you dividends.

Stock exchanges like the NYSE (New York Stock Exchange), NASDAQ, the Tokyo Stock Exchange are some of the largest exchanges. However, stocks are also sold in over-the-counter markets where they trade directly through brokers and not in open exchanges like the NYSE. These markets are referred to as secondary markets where investors trade stocks by buying and selling amongst themselves.

Basic Terms and Concepts

- **Stocks**

  A stock is a share of ownership in a company. Stocks are also referred to as shares. When you buy a stock you acquire a fraction of ownership of the company whose shares you have bought. When you buy stocks, you become a shareholder in a particular company and the percentage or size of your shares will determine the dividends you can earn.

Investors in the stock market can make money from their stocks in different ways. You can earn money in the form of dividends paid out on the shares you own. You can also earn money by selling your shares or stocks.

- **Common Stock**

Common stocks give you ownership of a company based on the number of shares you own. Common stocks are the most basic type of shares to own and they entitle you to dividends where applicable and voting rates proportionate to the shares you own.

- **Preferred Stock**

Preferred stocks entitle you to a fixed dividend rate for your shares. With this type of stock, you earn dividends before shareholders who have common stock but you do not get voting rights. Unlike shareholders of common stocks, preferred stocks give you a guarantee that you will receive dividends on your stock.

- **Penny Stocks**

A penny stock is a stock that trades for less than $5 per share. Penny stocks are typically short-term holdings where you want to take advantage of price movements in volatile markets. Penny stocks investing works for short-term investors who do not plan to hold the stocks for long periods.

- **Blue Chip Stocks**

Blue-chip stocks are shares of large established corporations that have solid reputations in the market. Blue-chip stocks are characterized by solid balance sheets and steady cash flows. Most blue-chip stocks have a history of earning increasing dividends for their shareholders. These types of stocks are ideal for long-term investors who want to hold stocks for long periods.

- **Primary Market**

In a primary market, companies sell their shares directly to investors. In most cases, companies in primary markets sell to corporations and institutions rather than to individual investors. Hedge funds, mutual funds, and similar investors are typically the kind of investors that buy shares directly from companies in primary markets.

- **Secondary Markets**

In a secondary market, investors buy and sell shares amongst themselves. Individual investors buy shares in secondary markets. In this type of market, you can choose to buy shares of a particular company or a mix of different companies' shares in exchange-traded funds or EFTs.

- **Over-the-Counter Markets**

OTC markets are where companies that are not listed in exchanges like NYSE trade their shares. In OTC markets there is no public price for the shares and the value of the transaction is dependent on the buyer and seller.

- **Bid**

A bid is a price at which you want to buy the share.

- **Ask**

The ask is the price at which the seller wants to sell the
share at

- **Spread**

The spread is the difference between the bids and sell
prices of a stock. If you want to buy a stock at $50
and the buyer wants to sell it at $45, the spread, in
this case, is $5.

- **Volatility**

Volatility refers to the movement of share prices in the
market. When the price fluctuates widely within short
periods of time then it is said to be highly volatile.
The higher the volatility of a particular share, the
higher the risk associated with it and also the higher
the profit potential.

- **Dividend**

A dividend is the percentage of a company's earnings that is paid out to shareholders. Dividends can be paid out annually or quarterly depending on the company. Not all companies pay dividends to the shareholders.

- **Broker**

A broker is a trader who buys and sells shares for an investor for a fee or commission.

- **Bear Market**

A bear market refers to a downward trend in the market where stock prices are falling

- **Bull Market**

A bull market refers to an upward trend in the market where stock prices are rising.

- **Beta**

Beta is the measurement of the price of a stock relative to the movement of the whole market. If a stock moves 1.5 points for every 1-point move in the market, then it has a beta of 1.5.

- **Index**

An index is a measure that is used as a benchmark to gauge market performance. Some of the most famous indices include the Dow Jones and the S&P 500.

Chapter 2. Steps to Evaluate Your Financial Health, Setting, Goals (What to Consider Before Opening a New Account)

There are many ways to go about investing and knowing which path to take can be a daunting process. You can narrow down the possibilities to a strategy that works for you by evaluating your current financial situation. This should be done before you enter into your first trade. To be successful, an investor needs a clear picture of where they are going. Keep in mind this is not a one-time event. You should reevaluate your financial situation on an annual basis since it's going to be changing. When you find yourself in a different financial situation, your investment strategies will change over time.

Where

Establishing a starting point is the first step. You don't have to be a financial wizard, but you need to be aware of your present situation before jumping in and buying stocks. Consider the following scenario. An investor with a large personal debt that has an interest rate of 17% keeps putting money in the stock market, hoping to build wealth over time. That sounds reasonable, but most market returns are, going to be in the range of 5-10%. That means that someone in this situation is actually losing money.

Seek Liquidity

We are going to recommend that you look for assets you can sell.

The money can be used to pay debts, back taxes, or to seed investment capital. You'll want to list all of your assets by liquidity, which means how easily they can be converted into cash. You'll also want to consider how much cash you can raise by selling each item if you were to sell it. A house might have a lot more value than a television set, but you might sell the television set in 24 hours while you'd have to wait months to sell the house.

Dealing with Debts

Taking care of debts is one of the first things that a budding investor needs to do. While you might be anxious to get started with a large-scale investment plan if you have debts to take care of you might want to put it off. So, the first step in preparing your investment plan is to create a simple balance sheet. You don't have to be an accountant, and you're only doing this for yourself, but it needs to be honest and accurate.

You're going to want to put together a listing of all of your assets and liabilities. When compiling assets, include everything of value that you could possibly sell. This could be a computer that you're not using, a dusty TV in a room nobody goes into very often, or an old guitar. Selling things, you don't need can help you pay off debts faster and raise investment capital. You might object that you wouldn't raise much money but imagine having an extra $500 to $1,000 to start off with.

When listing your liabilities, you're going to want to know how much debt you have, what the interest rates are, and what your monthly payments are.

Monthly payments are less important than interest rates. Once you've listed all of your debts, you'll want to develop a plan to pay them off in a reasonable amount of time. There are many calculators available online, and you can also read many books on how to pay off debt. The series of books by debt guru Dave Ramsey is highly recommended. Here is an example of a good debt calculator:

**https://www.creditkarma.com/calculators/
debt_repayment/**

You can use this calculator to figure out how long it will take to pay off a debt for a given monthly payment. You can enter the interest rate, and the time frame you would like along with the monthly payment you're willing to make. Start off with the current minimum payment in order to determine the time required to pay off the debt and work up from there.

In this example, we considered a $21,000 debt with a high 11% interest rate. Paying $450 a month would take five years to pay off the debt.

Additional Debt Repayment Information

Full Payoff

Balance	Interest Rate	Expected Monthly Payment	Expected Payoff Time
$21,000	11%	$450	62 months

Debt Repayment Chart

| Principal | $21,370 |
| Interest | $6,530 |

Click on the chart to see how much interest you will pay over the life of the debt.

That isn't a good situation to be in — do you want to saddle yourself with a $21,000 debt for five years?

36

When you have listed all of your debts, then you can prioritize them. In order to make the most progress in the shortest amount of time, it can be helpful to tackle the smallest debts first. This not only helps you get rid of your debt faster, but it will also have psychological benefits as you improve your financial situation.

If you have back taxes, you should make these a priority. The reason is that the government tacks on lots of fees and penalties, and if the tax debt is allowed to sit around, it can grow substantially in size. Get payment plans arranged to take care of these debts before they become unmanageable.

Take a look at your spending habits. Having material goods now isn't important if you plan to become a successful investor. You will be able to buy that BMW or Mercedes you want later when you can really afford it. For now, your focus should be on being able to direct your financial resources into your investments so that you can grow your wealth over time. Expensive toys, like a new car, can be a large financial drain. If you have car loans, consider getting out of the car and into a used car that is reliable but costs a lot less. From this point forward, don't use debt to finance purchases. Keep a credit card on hand for emergencies, but don't use it to buy things like books or groceries that should be paid for using cash. If you can't pay for something with cash, it can wait.

Having an Emergency Fund

Life is never fair, and we are all going to encounter emergencies.

Recent studies have shown that most Americans don't have enough cash on hand to pay a $500 bill. If you are in that situation, you need to rectify it before you jump in with a large-scale investment plan. Remember that paying off debt first is always the priority. Debt is a sink that sucks important financial resources down the drain that could be used for other purposes. However, it's important to start putting money away for an emergency fund to be prepared for the unexpected — and being able to pay for it without having to take on more debt. Or worse, getting into a situation where you can't get credit but still need to find money to pay emergency bills. Set aside a small amount of money that you can start depositing into a savings account that you won't touch unless there is an emergency. Over time, the goal should be to have enough cash on hand to take care of emergency bills ranging up to $5,000 and to have funds on hand to cover times when you might be unemployed.

Consider Additional Sources of Income

If you have a large amount of debt or find yourself in a situation where coming up with a significant amount of money to invest is difficult, you should consider taking action to increase your income. There are many paths to consider. You can start by looking for a higher-paying job.

Alternatively, you can look into taking a second job, at least until you are in a better financial situation. Another approach that can be used is to either take on "gigs" or short-term contract work.

This can be done online or by doing some side work with companies like Uber. You can even look into starting your own online business to generate more income.

This doesn't have to be a permanent situation, but you are going to want to get to a place where you are debt-free and can put $1,000 or more into the stock market every month.

Net Worth and Changes Over Time

When you've gathered everything together, you'll want to determine your net worth. You are doing this for yourself, so don't be embarrassed if it's in a bad position right now. Simply add up the total current value of your assets and liabilities and subtract the total value of the liabilities from the total value of your assets. This is your net worth. If you can compare the value of each asset now to the value it had at the beginning of the year; you can also calculate the change in your net worth in percentage terms.

Are You Ready to Invest?

If you are debt-free or have a plan in place to take care of your debts and to build an emergency fund, you are ready to begin investing. The first rule of investing is to never invest more than you can afford to lose. If you go about your investment plan carefully, the chances of losing everything are slim to none. That said it's a wise approach to invest as if that could really happen. So, you shouldn't be

40

investing next month's house payment or your kid's college funds in the hopes of gaining returns. After you have taken care of your debts and emergency fund, add up all of your basic living expenses, so you know how much you actually need per month. Anything left over above that is the amount of money you can invest for now.

Determining Your Financial Goals

Once you are in a position to invest something — even if you can only put in $100 a month now because you're paying off large debts — it's time to sit down and figure out your financial goals. There are several things to keep in mind:

Age: Generally speaking, the older you are, the more conservative you should be in your investment approach. The reason for this is simple. When things go badly, it takes time to recover and get back on the road to profitability. The older you are, the less time you have to grow your wealth in the future. That means a market crash, or a bad investment has larger consequences than it would have if you had thirty years to recover. Financial advisors generally recommend that older investors put their money in safer investments, which means putting some money into bonds and safe investments like US Treasuries that preserve capital. In the stock market, the older investor will seek out more stable companies that are larger, and while they may be growing, they have slow and steady growth with lower levels of risk. Of course, age can cut both ways. Many people reach their fifties with little to no savings or investment. If that describes your situation, you're going to want to invest more aggressively to seek rapid growth. Younger people also want to invest more aggressively, as they have a time horizon that permits taking on more risk. But time horizon isn't the only factor if you have no capital to protect; you definitely want to be more aggressive.

Chapter 3. Risks in Investing in Stocks

Understanding risk and volatility are two of the most important things to keep in mind with the stock market.

There are many different types of risk in the stock market. Some are direct, such as a small company that has the *potential* to make gains because of innovative products. Others are indirect and external. You can't manage all types of risks. Some come out of the blue, like the 9/11 terrorist attacks or the 2008 financial crash. So, if you think that you can control every form of risk, take a deep breath and realize you can't. In this chapter, we are going to try and describe every major category of risk investor's face, and if possible, we'll suggest ways to deal with them.

Emotional and Person Risk

First and foremost, you can control the risks to your investments that come from personal factors. These include fear, impatience, and greed. Emotions like these can be hard to control, but learning to take charge of them is essential if you are going to be a successful investor.

When real money is on the line, these emotions can become strong and overpowering. You must not let that happen.

The most common problem when it comes to emotions and personal risk is fear. When a stock market starts looking bearish, many investors immediately jump ship. They are making a huge mistake. A good investor is not getting in and out of the market at the slightest sign of a problem. In fact, selling off when everyone else is could be one of the biggest mistakes individual investors make. By the way, that doesn't exempt large investors. Many professional traders are subject to the same emotions and exhibit the same behavior during downturns. Massive selloffs are what cause bear markets to develop.

First of all, remember that you are looking to hold your investments over the long term. So, the ups and downs of the market and even recessions are not a reason to sell them. Over the past 50 years, by far the worst stock market contraction happened in the 2008 financial crisis. However, even that was short-lived. People that sold off their investments were either faced with being out of the markets altogether or having to get back in the markets when prices were appreciating. The lifetimes of other major bear markets were similar or even more short-lived. The first lesson in managing personal risk is to hold your investments through downturns.

The second lesson is that rather than giving into fear, you should start to see market downturns as opportunities. When prices are rapidly dropping due to a market sell-off, you should be buying shares. It's impossible to know where the bottom of a market is, and you shouldn't concern yourself with that.

At any time that share prices are declining, it's an opportunity, and so you should be making regular stock purchases. In one year, two years, or five years down the road, on average, the stocks that you purchased in a downturn are going to be worth quite a bit more.

The second problem that arises as a part of personal risk is greed. Many people start seeing dollar signs when they begin investing. Having a get-rich-quick mentality is not compatible with successful investing. Your approach should be centered on slowly and steadily accumulating wealth and not making a quick buck. As you invest, you're going to be coming across claims that certain trades or stocks are the next best thing, but you're better off ignoring such claims. More often than not, they turn out to be false. The stock market is not a gambling casino, even though many people treat it that way. You can avoid succumbing to greed by maintaining a regular investment program and not being taken in by the temptation that you can profit from short-term swings or "penny stocks" that are going to supposedly take off.

Finally, there is the related problem of impatience. After the Great Depression, people developed a more reasonable and cautious approach to the stock market. They realized that you're not going to get rich in six months or a year. The idea of long-term investing became dominant.

Unfortunately, in recent years, this lesson seems to be getting lost. More people are behaving like traders rather than as investors. Far too many investors are being taken in by the seduction of being able to beat market returns. Instead of being impatient, you should realize that you're in it for the long haul. Rather than trying to make a few extra bucks now, you're seeking to build wealth.

Risk of Loss of Capital

Obviously, financial risk is something you face when investing. Theoretically, there is a chance that you will lose all the money you invest in the stock market. This can happen if you tie your fate to a small number of companies. Several well-known companies like Lumber Liquidators, Bear-Stearns, and GM have either had major problems or gone completely under. Investors may have lost large sums in the process. The way to deal with this is to avoid investing in a small number of companies. Later in the chapter, we will investigate diversification as an investment strategy.

You'll also want to pay attention to the types of companies you invest in. Putting all of your money into small-cap stocks, for example, is probably a bad idea. So is putting all of your money into emerging markets, or into one sector of the stock market. Again, the key message is diversification. It's the way to protect you from financial risk.

Market and Economic Risk

Some factors are beyond your control, and the economy inevitably cycles through slowdowns and downturns. The market will cycle along with the economy, and also experience crashes when the economy may be doing fine overall. This happened in 1987, for example.

While these factors are not under your control, how you react to them is under your control. As we discussed in the section on emotional risk, you should not panic when there is a downturn. Remain level-headed, and use downturns as a buying opportunity. They are always followed by a brighter day; your job is to have the patience to wait for it to arrive.

Interest Rate Risk

Changing interest rates can impact the markets. Although this is a book about stock market investing, you should have some awareness of how bond markets work. You should also be aware that investor money can flow back and forth between bond and stock markets depending on conditions.

One thing that bond markets offer is the safety of capital, especially when we are talking about U.S. government bonds. When interest rates are high, U.S. government bonds (and other types of bonds, including corporate and municipal bonds) become very attractive.

Interest rate changes have risks for bond investors, however. Bonds are traded on secondary markets. When interest rates rise, bond prices fall because older bonds that offer lower interest rates become less attractive. Conversely, when interest rates fall, older bonds that pay higher interest rates have more value than new bonds being issued that pay relatively low rates.

This doesn't directly affect a stock market investor, but if demand for bonds rises, that can mean less capital flowing into the stock market. Less demand means lower prices, so the market may see declines.

Also, as we'll see, you can invest in bonds through the stock market using exchange-traded funds. If you are using this method, you'll want to keep close tabs on interest rates. That means paying closer attention to the Federal Reserve and its quarterly announcements. You should be doing so even if you are not going to invest in bonds in any way.

Announcements on interest rate changes can have a large impact on stock prices. But as always, keep your eye on the long ball. If the markets react negatively to an increase in interest rates that can be an opportunity to buy undervalued stocks.

Political Risk and Government

Government and politics can create big risks in the stock market. International events can cause market crashes, and these days even a tweet from the President can cause markets to rise and fall. Lately, some politicians have also been discussing breaking up the big tech companies. Others are talking about investigating them. Such talk — and worse actions— can have a negative impact on the markets. Part of your job as an investor is to keep a close eye on the news. You're going to want to know what's happening so that you can adjust if necessary.

Inflation Risk

Inflation hasn't been high in decades. However, in the late 1970s inflation rates were routinely in the double digits. Hopefully, that isn't going to be something that happens anytime soon, because high inflation rates can eat your returns alive. If the stock market is appreciating at 7% per year, but inflation is 14%, you can see that it's like having debt but investing in stocks — it's a losing proposition. Right now, inflation risk is very low, but you'll want to have some awareness of it and always keep tabs on it. High inflation rates also tend to go hand-in-hand with high interest rates, since the Federal Reserve will raise rates to try and slow down inflation. That means that bonds might become more attractive when inflation gets out of control.

Taxes and Commissions

Finally, we have the risk imposed by taxes. Of course, we are all going to be hit with taxes no matter where our money comes from. However, you need to take into account the taxes that you are going to pay when it comes to any gains you realize on the stock market. Part of being a successful investor is having an understanding of how much your taxes are cutting into your profits. If you are investing for the long-term, it will be less of an issue. But keep in mind that taxes can really eat into short-term trades. Frequent, short-term traders also face risk from commissions and fees. If you execute a lot of trades, the commissions can add up. This is not an issue for long-term investors.

Risk vs. Return

One of the fundamental trade-offs that an investor will make is risk vs. return. Generally speaking, the higher the risk, the greater the *possibility* of good returns. In 1998, Amazon was a pretty high-risk investment. While it had potential, major bookstores like Borders and Barnes & Noble dominated the space. Amazon was on shaky ground at the time, and another company could have come in and competed successfully for online book sales. That never happened, and Amazon ended up dominating book sales and expanding widely across retail and into cloud computing. That risk has translated into massive returns. A $10,000 investment in 1998 would be worth more than $1 million today.

But hindsight is 20/20. Today, there are similar opportunities all around us, but it's hard to know which ones will end up being successful over the long term. If you are an aggressive investor, part of your job will be estimating which companies are the best bets for the future.

These examples serve to illustrate why a diversified portfolio is essential.

Managing Risk

There are a few time-tested strategies that have been developed that help manage risk. They even minimize, as much as possible, the kinds of risk that you will face that are completely out of control. That could include anything from a terrorist attack to interest rate changes.

These strategies are simple and easy to understand. The problem is that in practice, many investors fail to follow them, and instead let their decision-making be guided by emotions. You might end up following that path as well. However, we are going to give you the tools you need to avoid it. It's up to you whether you utilize them or not.

Chapter 4. How to Invest in Stocks

(How to Buy Your First Stock)

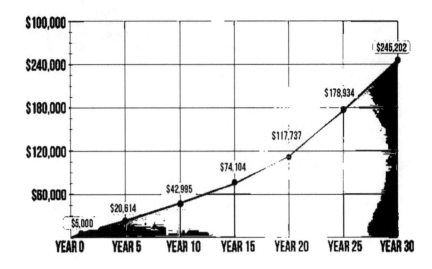

How to Get Start

Stock may seem incredibly intimidating for those starting in the investment world. It looks like a completely different world, and the hardest step for most is the beginning. However, it is quite simple to get started in stock investments. First, one must set goals for themselves and determine how they would like to invest in a stock. By writing down goals and ensuring that the investor's money is used in the best possible way, the investor is helping them yield the highest return on their investment. Once the individual's goals are made clear, they must plan on how to meet those goals. After this, they may choose the best investment method for achieving these goals. Then, it must be decided on where exactly the investor will go to invest their money. It is crucial, as this will be the platform by which the investor will trade their stocks. After this, the investor must open an account with whomever they choose. Before they start trading, the investor must make an initial investment using this account. While doing so, they may have to link their bank account to their stock trading account. The investor must then begin the process of buying and selling stocks using this account. Although this seems like a lengthy process, it is quite simple.

Planning and Meeting Goals

Investors must familiarize themselves with their goals. It is quite helpful to write down one's goals in each area and put them somewhere that is easily accessible. It is useful to have measurable goals to reach. This way, there may be a specific period and amount that may be assigned to the targets. It may help to come up with monthly goals. For instance, the investor may start with the purchase of 100 shares of stock in February. They may wish to increase that to 150 shares by March, 200 shares by April, and so on. This way, the investor may have a period to achieve their goals. It will allow them to measure their progress easily.

To set proper goals, one must reflect upon their past. How much will the investor be able to set aside for stock realistically? If one's goals are not realistic, it may become discouraging and set the investor back from their full potential. The investor must consider any past investments they have made. They must consider what worked and what did not. It is crucial to consider income and expenses when investing, and one must also consider any savings goals that one has. This will make it more apparent what may be invested in stocks.

Without a clear guide on how to invest, the investor will lack direction. It may lead to spur-of-the-moment decisions, and the investor may regret these choices. There may be some periods where one will not trade, as it won't be as profitable. Perhaps the market is down, and the trader does not wish to sell any stock. Perhaps the market is up, and the trader does not want to buy any stock. There will be events such as vacations, holidays, stressful events, or emergencies.

One must also consider how much money they have. Although it is possible to double one's money in a year, it is not likely for a beginner to do so. One may also choose to invest one time and hold it, or they may choose to invest more into their account often. This time and amount will depend on the investor and their financial situation.

The investor must also choose a strategy. They may wish to buy and sell stocks or to buy and hold stocks. They may even consider options trading. Whichever method that the investor chooses, there will be different goals to fit those strategies.

Long-term goals may be set to help the investor. Although planning for the following year may help the investor, longer periods may prove even more beneficial. Perhaps the investor wishes to acquire a million dollars worth of stock in the succeeding ten years. Perhaps the investor wishes to save a certain amount for retirement, which they wish to have by the next 25 years. Whatever the end goal is, the investor must make that clear so that they can begin working towards it immediately. Once a proper plan is created for meeting the investor's goals, they may move to the next step.

Choosing an Investment Method

After the investor has set goals and created a plan to meet them, it is time to decide on which investment method they wish to pursue. For those that wish to trade on their own completely, the DIY (do-it-yourself) method is the best fit. The investor may conduct all their trades online, making transfers from the bank manually or automatically. It will allow full control of one's investments. There will also be complete independence over what the investor wishes to buy and sell, how much they wish to trade, and how often they wish to trade.

They will, however, need to dedicate time to researching, making any transfers, trading, and other procedures. There is also a higher risk for this choice, as a beginning investor will not have the education that a financial advisor will. They also won't be under the control of a Robo-Advisor. However, all the profit that is made by the investor will be theirs to keep. They won't have to pay commission and fees outside of any required by the broker that they use.

The least independent approach to investing in stock is by hiring a financial advisor. It is for those who do not wish to touch their stock at all and to have it fully regulated for them. Hesitant beginners may benefit from this method. It is important to remember, however, that this method tends to be the costliest. It is most beneficial for those with higher assets and larger portfolios. It is also important to choose an investor that will work to meet the investor's goals, not just the goals of themselves. Therefore, the investor must set specific goals for themselves and how they wish to invest their money. They may more easily communicate with the advisor their desires, which may be carried out for them.

Choosing a Stockbroker

When investing for oneself, a proper stockbroker must be chosen. This will depend on the individual's needs and wants. For some, their bank that they already operate offers stock investments through their bank. This is a quick and simple option, as their money will already be linked through the bank, and they may already be familiar with their style. There may also be options for financial advisors in the bank that are free of charge. Otherwise, the investor must research their options before settling on a broker.

When choosing a stockbroker, the investor should research any fees (transaction fees, maintenance fees, etc.), minimum funds required to open an account, any commission collected by the stockbroker, and accessibility. The investor may prefer a specific type of formatting for their broker to have. There may also be free education, customer service, and other ways to make investing easier for the investor.

The investor must choose the option that will allow them to make the highest return on their investments. The investor should keep in mind which services they are likely to use most frequently, and they should choose the broker that charges the least to use those services. There may be transactional fees, which are costs for buying and selling stocks. Many beginning investors tend to forget this, so it is essential to take this into account.

Opening an Account

When opening an account, there are often a few steps that are required. This is typically not a lengthy process, but the investor should be aware of the potential actions associated with opening an account.

The first step when opening an online account is typically to create an account. This will consist of a username and password, as well as some personal information. This may include setting goals, determining which types of features the investor wishes to use, and the investor's experience level. This information will help to create the optimal experience for the investor.

There may also be an application for the account to ensure that the investor is qualified to hold the account. There may also be an agreement stating that the investor assumes all the risks of investing and understands that the money is not insured or guaranteed. Initial Investment and Linking Accounts

During the application process, the investor will most likely be prompted to fund the account. This can be done in several ways. The investor may transfer the funds electronically via an EFT (Electronic funds transfer). This is transferring the money from a linked bank account and will most likely only take one business day to transfer. The investor may also choose to make a wire transfer, which is a transfer directly from the bank. It is important to consider how much to invest in the account initially carefully. For those just starting, there may not be much money to invest at first. The minimum investment amounts for the broker should be looked over beforehand.

Buying and Selling Stocks

After the investor funds their account, it is time to start trading the stocks. It must be decided what stock, how much of the stock, and how the investor wishes to buy. Once these factors are decided, the investor must buy the stock. It is usually as simple as searching the stock symbol and selecting "buy." It is best to wait until the stock is at a low, but the investor must also begin investing as early as possible in experiencing the benefits of investing. When the stock is bought, it will typically take a bit to process and for the broker to receive these funds. After that, it will show up in the online portfolio of the investor. When it is time to sell this stock, the investor may typically visit their portfolio and click "sell" on the desired stock.

Chapter 5. When to Buy and Sell Stock

When to Sell a Stock

Determining when to sell a stock is a decision that even the world's best investors wrestle with. Warren Buffett has said that his holding period for a stock is forever. Does Buffett really hold every stock that he buys forever? Of course not! The point that he is making is that you should always purchase a stock with the intention of holding it forever; therefore, make sure your money has been put into your best investment ideas. An investor should leave his or her portfolio intact for at least five years, as long as the fundamentals for which a particular stock was purchased do not deteriorate. Investors should pay no attention to a stock's price volatility because it is a normal part of the investment cycle. As a long-term investor, there will be times when it makes sense to sell or reduce your position in stock earlier than you had planned. Next, we will talk about different circumstances in which you should consider selling a stock or reducing your position in a stock.

- **The Time Frame** — If you need the money within five years, it should not be invested in stocks. It would be best to invest your money in safe and stable short-term instruments. Money market accounts, money market funds, and short-term certificates of deposits would be better options. Since the Great Recession struck, some investment professionals now recommend that you not invest any money in stocks that will be needed within 10 years.

- **An Overvalued Stock** — When a stock is significantly overvalued, sell it. Take the proceeds from the sale and invest them into other undervalued stocks that you have researched. The P/E ratio is still one of the best indicators of value. For example, if a stock has traded at an average P/E of 15 for the last seven to 10 years and the business is thriving, but the stock currently trades at a P/E of 30 or more on consistent or increasing EPS, you should seriously consider selling the stock. The PEG ratio is also a very effective method for determining if a stock is now overvalued.

- **Too Much Debt** — Too much debt is dangerous for any business because there's always the chance that a business may be unable to pay its debt. Too much debt also puts a business at greater risk of failure if a downturn in the industry or economy were to occur. Upon entering the 2007 recession, thousands of businesses here in the United States literally disappeared overnight and that was before things really got bad.

- **Too Much Risk** — You have already learned the importance of staying away from investments that are too risky. Sometimes new management will come to a business and begin to implement new policies; along with that implementation, they will knowingly or unknowingly expose a business to greater risk. If you purchased the stock of a business that stayed away from very risky practices, but the business has now begun to display risky behaviors that make you uncomfortable, sell the stock and find yourself a better investment.

- **Loss of Competitive Advantage** — You have also learned that we should only be purchasing the stocks of businesses that have a durable competitive advantage. When a business changes its business model, resulting in it losing its competitive advantage, sell the stock.

- **The Portfolio Lacks Balance or Diversification** — It's very easy for your best performing stock to become the largest holding in your portfolio, and there's absolutely nothing wrong with that. The problem arises when the stock makes up more than 20-25% of your portfolio's total value. Legendary investor, Jim Slater suggests that individual investors limit the number of funds invested in a single stock within their portfolios to a maximum of 15%. When your portfolio becomes heavily weighted in one stock, consider reducing your position of that stock to bring more balance and better diversification into your portfolio.

- **Stock Reaches Its Fair Value** — Our goal as investors should always be to purchase a stock at a discount to its fair value and it is recommended at least a 25% discount to its fair value. By doing so, when you sell a stock that has reached its fair value, you are guaranteed a gain of at least 25% from the sale. This is a disciplined approach to selling a stock.

According to research, it was common for Benjamin Graham to sell a stock once it had a 50% gain in price. If the future prospects of a particular stock look good, you may decide to sell only a portion of the stock, such as half of its shares, and hold on to the rest when using this approach.

- **When Your Analysis is Found to Be Flawed**—
There will be times when an investor will be very detailed and careful in his or her analysis of a particular company or its stock, only to find out later that his or her analysis is incorrect or flawed. Whether a stock should be sold at that time depends on the seriousness of the error and its impact on the long-term performance of the business. So, when you find that you have incorrectly analyzed a particular business, it is essential for you to take a serious look at all available information to determine whether or not to sell the stock or to continue holding it. One thing is certain, as an investor, you will not always be right when analyzing a company or its stock.

There is no clear-cut way to determine the optimal time to sell a stock. There will be times that you will sell a stock because it has not performed well, only to see it skyrocket and double or triple in price soon after you sell it. There will also be occasions when you have purchased what seems to be the perfect stock, only to watch it tumble in price and for no apparent reason. Learn what you can from these events and move on. Even Peter Lynch, Jim Slater, and other great investors have sold stocks too early or too late. It's going to happen sometimes.

When to Buy a Stock

After the investor funds their account, it is time to start trading the stocks. It must be decided what stock, how much of the stock, and how the investor wishes to buy. Once these factors are decided, the investor must buy the stock. It is usually as simple as searching the stock symbol and selecting "buy." It is best to wait until the stock is at a low, but the investor must also begin investing as early as possible in experiencing the benefits of investing. When the stock is bought, it will typically take a bit to process and for the broker to receive these funds. After that, it will show up in the online portfolio of the investor. When it is time to sell this stock, the investor may typically visit their portfolio and click "sell" on the desired stock.

Starting out as a stock investor is quite simple. The investor must follow a few steps to become a stock trader. They must choose an investment method, select a stockbroker, open an account, a fund that account, and they will be ready to go.

Your very first stock trade can be frightening - not to mention confounding. You've done your stock research, you believe you've found a winner, and now you're all set to put your brand-new brokerage account to excellent usage and begin trading — nevertheless, you're not quite sure how to "carry it out."

Trade "execution" is just an elegant technique for describing an exchange. To "trade" typically describes a particular kind of investing method, so certifying your use of the term "trade" with "carry out" lets other financiers understand that you're going over a particular exchange.

The real-time it takes to perform your trade can move from broker to broker and market to market. (The SEC requires that all brokerage companies supply documents quarterly to the basic population about the handling of their customer orders).

Your broker will unquestionably put your order through their complicated trading computer system network to get a hold of your shares when you do put in your order. In many cases, your order will never ever leave the broker — your brokerage company ought to clean out shares of the organization you're purchasing from its stock.

You have a couple of choices when it comes to trading stocks beyond merely selling and purchasing. Basically, you get shares of a particular stock and sell them, relying on that the stock will diminish in worth, leaving the distinction between the selling rate and ultimate repurchase rate in your pocket.

Stock Order Types

Naturally, buying stocks is similarly more complex than only one purchase. There are numerous different approaches for considering your purchase, all going concerning cost, the time point of confinement, which is simply the start.

Anyhow, what are your alternatives for purchasing stock? There are 5 various types of stock orders that your broker will likely let you utilize.

A market order is a demand to sell a stock or buy at the existing market value. Market orders are quite a great deal for the basic stock order, and because the capability is typically performed instantly.

Something to keep as a primary top priority with a market order is the way you do not manage the amount you pay for your stock purchase or sale; the marketplace does.

The speed with which online market orders have actually launched might have made this less of a danger than it used to be. The market still moves quicker.

Some individuals do not have problems with this, for those that do this, imperfection can be met with a breaking point order.

- **Point of Confinement Order**

A breaking point order can keep you from purchasing or selling your stock at a rate that you do not want, possibly assisting you in keeping a strategic range from a horrible choice. On the off possibility that the cost is a misdirected base and not in tune with the market, nevertheless, the order will never ever be made.

Keep in mind that some brokers charge more for point of confinement orders, as the trade might not go through.

- **Stop-loss Order**

Stop-loss orders, when that price is reached, transform into market orders. The target price is hit, and the trade is executed at market value.

- **Stop-Limit Order**

Stop-limit orders are also stopped orders based on hanging tight at a particular expense. Stop-limit orders end up being point of confinement orders when the target cost is reached as opposed to market orders.

Changing into a breaking point order can be something useful for a stop order, staying away from particular threats. On the occasion that the shares topple to $20.00 at the very same time, then instantly shoot back up, your market order might go through in any case.

- **Tracking Stop**

Generally, this is a stop order based upon a portion modification in the market cost instead of setting a target cost.

You can pick to what degree the order stays open when you put an order into your broker. Naturally, orders are day orders, indicating that they are signed up until completion of the trading day. Outstanding till-canceled orders stay open until you really enter and cancel them.

Chapter 6. How to Generate Passive Income from the Stock Market

Income investing is a little bit of a different ballgame than growth investing. In this case, we are seeking out companies that pay dividends. That means ignoring a lot of high growth stocks like Amazon and Netflix. It also means ignoring disruptive companies with potential like Tesla. When you are an income investor, you are looking to make a certain level of income from your stock holdings. That may be now, or it may be in the future. But your portfolio is going to look quite different from a growth investor, and even a value-oriented growth investor.

Yield

Start compiling a diverse list of companies that pay dividends that you find interesting. In each case, track the yield, which is the dividend divided by the share price. That will help you compare apples-to-apples when judging one dividend stock against another. Keep in mind that you are going to be seeking some kind of balance, so buying up stocks with the highest yields isn't the best philosophy. To see why to consider a company called consolidated communications. They pay a yield of 32%. The problem is, it's a penny stock. That means it's only $4 or so a share.

Most analysts are rating it a SELL. A glance at the chart indicates it has dropped from a $29 share price over the past couple of years, and yet it's still rated as being overvalued. These are major red flags.

Dividend

You may also be interested in the actual dividend payment, and not just the yield. IBM pays $6 a share, but Apple only pays $1.55 a share. So, you'd have to own more than three Apple shares for every share of IBM you could buy in order to get the same annual income from your stocks. Since IBM is cheaper on a per-share basis, that is something to take into consideration.

Dividend Growth

For any stock that you invest in, you're going to want to look at the history of their dividend payments. The ideal dividend stock is one that pays higher dividends over time. IBM is a great example because they paid consistent dividends through the 2008 financial crisis, and they have been increasing their dividends since then. Dividend growth ensures that your dividend payments will keep up with or exceed inflation.

DRIPS and Reinvesting

If you have a large amount of capital available right now, you can buy up shares of stock and start living off the dividend payments. However, if you are looking at a long-term investment program, you are going to want to reinvest your dividends. In the future, you're going to want to have as many shares as possible, so taking cash out now simply doesn't make sense. Instead, the payments from dividends should be used to purchase additional shares. Some companies even allow you to purchase fractional shares with the money.

A DRIP is a Dividend Reinvestment Program. In this case, the company will automatically take any dividends you earn and use them to buy additional shares. This will help enforce discipline in case you get tempted to cash out your dividends and waste the money on a trip or new car. Instead, the company will force you to save for the future.

Exchange-Traded Funds

The possibility of using exchange-traded funds to meet your investment goals always exists. In this case, you can seek out an ETF that invests in dividend stocks. You will still receive dividend payments, and the fund will have built-in diversification. When looking at ETFs to use for dividend investing, be sure to focus on yield, and pick funds that have the highest yields. Many investors can do a mixture of both; you could invest in ETFs while also investing in specific companies like IBM.

Alternative Investments

The world of dividend investing isn't restricted to traditional stock investing. You can also invest in the following:

- REITS

- MLPs

- BDCs

A REIT is a real estate trust. This is a company that owns hard property assets and rents them out. The types of property are quite varied. For example, you can invest in

REITs that own rental homes, apartments, or commercial real estate. There are also REITs that own hotels and resorts. In fact, any type of property that you can think of is represented by at least one REIT. But interestingly, there are REITs that have great prospects for the future because they are technology-related. For example, some REITs own cell phone towers, and there are others that own cloud computing.

REITs pay high dividends, and they trade like stocks on the stock market. Investing in REITs is a good way to get some exposure to real estate and other types of property ownership.

An MLP is a master limited partnership. These companies are midstream energy companies that transport oil and gas, own pipelines, or own refinement facilities. These are great investments to consider, and they also pay high dividends. You also invest in them by purchasing shares on the stock market. These types of investments are particularly noteworthy because the companies are partnerships and not corporations. When you invest, you become a limited partner. This means that you can deduct company expenses on your tax returns. Essentially, a large share of the income from an MLP is tax-free.

The final alternative investment that we are looking at is called a BDC, or Business Development Corporation. They also trade on stock exchanges and pay dividends. These are financial companies that invest in small to mid-sized companies that need cash. They can provide loans to companies or take an ownership stake.

When to Cash Out

Cashing out is a personal decision. By cashing out, in this case, we don't mean selling off your shares. What we mean is when should you stop reinvesting and start taking dividends as cash income. The answer is you start doing this when the level of dividend payments you receive starts matching your desired income.

Don't be afraid to shake up your portfolio. If you find an investment that suits your needs better than stocks you are currently invested in, then you should be ready to sell some of your shares and invest in the other stock. There is no reason for you to be locked into a particular stock, you can buy shares in other companies and then start getting dividend payments from them in the next upcoming cycle.

Fundamentals Always Matter

No matter which path you choose, when dividend investing, you want to pay close attention to the fundamentals. In the end, fundamentals are what matters. A company with good fundamentals is going to be a good investment. So, you'll want some trade-off between solid fundamentals, yield, and dividend payment that suits your goals. Remember to always think long-term.

Bond Investing

Finally, if you are looking for an income investing portfolio, consider buying exchange-traded funds that invest in bonds.

As we discussed earlier, there is a wide array of choices, allowing you to find the right amount of risk and the right interest payments. You'll want to look at the yields of the bond funds. Some have high rates of growth and high yields. That is, you can achieve growth as well as income by investing in bond funds too. The advantage of using ETFs is that you can avoid the hassle of trying to invest in bond markets.

Chapter 7. The Main Mistakes of a Beginner

Mistakes happen in every field, sector, and industry. Some are always anticipated, while others happened unexpectedly. When it comes to stock trading, there are several mistakes that you can make. Understanding these mistakes can help you avoid them, thus ending up successful in your stock investments. Here are some of the common mistakes made by most investors, beginners, and professional traders alike:

Failure to Understand the Trade

It is always wrong to invest in a trade or business you know nothing about. It is a great mistake to engage in stock trading when you do not understand the business and financial models involved. You can avoid this mistake by taking the time to research the stock market and stock trading before investing your money. Know the different markets, the driving forces, as well as trading procedures.

Most investors tend to buy stocks from the latest companies and industries they know very little about. Although such companies may look promising, it is difficult to determine whether they will continue to exist. Understanding a specific company gives you a better hand over other investors. You will be able to make accurate predictions about the company or industry, which may bring you more profit. You will quickly tell when the business is booming, stagnating, or closing way before other investors get this information.

Individuals who do not take time to study companies miss out on future trends of these companies. Failing to establish such trends leads to several missed opportunities. For instance, a person who invests in a company that is higher than his capital may quickly lose all his investment. That is why it is always advisable that you invest in the industry you understand better. For instance, if you are a surgeon, you can invest in stocks that deal with medicine or related stocks. Lawyers can invest in companies that generate income through litigation, and so on.

Impatience

The stock market is for patient investors. It is a slow but steady form of investment. Although it bears various opportunities that can bring you money, you cannot make enough profit in one day. Most stock investors are always faced with the challenge of being patient. Some end up losing trade positions before they mature in the quest to make quick money. Exiting the market too early will always cost you some returns. As a new investor, you must never expect your investment portfolio to perform more than its capability, as this will always lead to a disaster. Remain realistic in terms of the time, duration, and resources needed to earn from the market.

Failure to Diversify

Another mistake that easily causes disaster is the failure to diversify. Professional investors do not have a problem with this since they can easily profit from a single type of stock. However, young investors must be able to diversify to secure their investment. Some of them do not stick to this principle. Most of these lose a great fortune as soon as they get onto the stock market. As you seek to invest, remember the rule of thumb governing stock diversity. This states that you should not invest more than 10% of your capital in one type of stock.

Getting Too Connected with a Certain Company

The essence of trading in stock is to make a profit. Sometimes, investors get too deep into a certain company that they forget that it is all about the shares and not the company itself. Being too attached to a company may cloud your judgment when it comes to stock trading since you may end up buying stocks from this company instead of getting the best deal on the market. As you learn more about companies, always remember that you are into the business to make money, besides creating relationships.

Investment Turnover

Investment turnover refers to the act of entering and exiting positions at will. This is one other mistake that destroys great investments. It is only beneficial to institutions that seek to benefit from low commission rates. Most stock trading positions charge transaction fees. The more frequently you buy and sell, the more you pay in terms of transaction fees. You, therefore, need to be careful when entering positions. Do not get in or exit too early. Have a rough idea of when you want to close positions so that you do not miss some of the long-term benefits of these positions.

Timing the Market

Market timing results in high investment turnover. It is not easy to successfully time the market. On average, only 94% of stock trading returns are acquired without the use of market timing. Most traders time the market as a way of attempting to recover their losses. They want to get even by making some profit to counter a loss. This is always known as a cognitive error in behavioral finance. Trying to get even on the stock market will always result in double losses.

Trading with Emotions

Allowing your emotions to rule is one of the things that kill your stock investment returns. Most people get into the market for fear of losses or thirst to make returns too fast. As a young trader, you must ensure that greed and fear do not overwhelm your decision-making. Stock prices may fluctuate a lot in the short-term; however, this may not be the case in the long term, especially for large-cap stocks.

This means that you may get lower profits in the short term, but these may increase in the long term. Understanding this will help you avoid closing trades when it is not the right time yet.

Setting Unrealistic Expectations

This always occurs when dealing with small-cap stocks such as penny stocks. Most investors buy such stocks with the expectation that the prices will change drastically. Sometimes this works, but it is not a guarantee. To make great fortunes, people invest a lot of capital in these stocks, and then the prices do not change much. If these investors are not prepared for such an eventuality, they may feel frustrated and may quit the business completely. However, this is something that you must be able to manage if you want to grow your investment. Do not expect more than what a certain type of stock can deliver.

Using Borrowed Money

This is probably one of the greatest mistakes that investors make. Some investors get carried away with the returns they are making. As a way of getting more profits, they borrow money and use it to enter more stock positions. This is a very dangerous move and can result in a lot of stress. Stock trading is like gambling. You are not always sure how much you take home at the end of each trade. It is therefore not advisable for you to invest borrowed money in it.

As you try to avoid these mistakes, you must also avoid getting information from the wrong sources. Some traders have lost a fortune because they relied on the wrong sources for stock information. It is important to isolate a small number of people and places where you will seek guidance from. Do not be a person that follows the crowd. Take time before investing in new stock opportunities. Carry out proper due diligence, especially with small-cap stocks since these involve a lot of risks. Remember, you must trade carefully and implement expert advice if you want to succeed in stock trading.

Conclusion

There are also many different types of investments, orders, and such that the individual may make. It is crucial that the investor knows the differences between these and can decide on which methods the investor wishes to invest in. However, the investor must know the pros and cons of each to reach that conclusion. The investor must educate himself or herself before making any further decisions on their investments and strategies for trading. There are many elements of the stock market that one must familiarize themselves with; the more that you know, the better the chance of you receiving a high return on your investment is.

Stock market investing can be very powerful for any person looking to create wealth or build a side income. Among all the asset classes, stock investments have generated the best returns historically. Consequently, it is beneficial for you over the long term that you develop a sound understanding of this highly profitable investment avenue.

The next step is to follow this through and begin your quest as a stock investor. It is important to begin by setting goals for yourself as an investor. You must consider all of the variables involved in investing. Setting goals will help provide you with a sense of direction. By using this as a reference, you may decide on which path of investing you will choose. What will be the time period of your investment? Will you purchase individual stocks or ETFs? How much risk are you willing to take in your investments? These questions, among others, must be answered to provide you with clear goals in your investing. After this, you may create an account, fund your account, and start trading. There must be research done, and you must select your stocks. After this, you are on the path to success in trading.

After you have accomplished this, you must continue to conduct research on the market, monitor your stocks, and manage your portfolio. Being an investor is an ongoing process. This can really help you to get started in learning about stock, and it may serve as a reference guide throughout your stock investing career. There will constantly be changes in the economy, the stock market will fluctuate every day, and the stocks themselves will continuously move. However, the basic concepts of stock will always be helpful to know, and this provides its readers with those basics that are necessary for one to be successful in stock investing.

The goal is to help investors, especially those who are just getting started with investing in the stock market, to learn the basic concepts of the stock market that will help them to initiate the trading process and become both successful and profitable in their investments.

Stock investing requires discipline, patience, and thoughtful analysis. Diversification is an essential strategy for successful stock investing. Keeping your emotions in check is also a crucial part of becoming a successful investor. A long-term approach to stock investments provides many times good returns.

By reading it to the end, you are proving that you are disciplined and ready to work hard! Many rookie investors spend their money investing blindly. Unlike the majority, you have taken your time to acquire knowledge to make wise decisions. Good job!

CPSIA information can be obtained
at www.ICGtesting.com
Printed in the USA
LVHW051049230621
690925LV00008B/758